JEREMY

CHRIS FAILLE · DANNY SNELL

working title press
An imprint of HarperCollins*Children's Books*

For all the birds that I tried to save as a child - D.S

Working Title Press
An imprint of HarperCollins*Children'sBooks*, Australia

First published in Australia in 2013
by Publishing Design Studio Pty Ltd
This edition published in 2018
by HarperCollins*Publishers* Australia Pty Limited
ABN 36 009 913 517
harpercollins.com.au

Text copyright © Christopher Faille 2013
Illustrations copyright © Danny Snell 2013

HarperCollins*Publishers*
Level 13, 201 Elizabeth Street, Sydney NSW 2000, Australia
Unit D1, 63 Apollo Drive, Rosedale, Auckland 0632, New Zealand

A catalogue record for this book is available from the National Library of Australia

ISBN 978 1 9215 0450 1

Designed and set in Corona by Liz Nicholson, design BITE
Danny Snell used acrylic paints on board for the illustrations in this book
Colour reproduction by Graphic Print Group, Adelaide
Printed and bound in China by RR Donnelley on 128gsm Matt Art

6   22

Last year a pair of kookaburras made a nest
high in the big palm tree in our garden.

One night our cat brought a baby bird
into the lounge room.

It was very ugly, with a big beak,
big bulgy closed eyes and no feathers.

It was a baby kookaburra.

It must have fallen out of the nest in the palm tree.
We couldn't put it back because the nest was too high.

We put the baby bird in a box and kept it warm with a hot water bottle.

We named it Jeremy.

Jeremy loved to eat.

We got some special food for baby kookaburras and we fed him every four hours. He grew very quickly.

After one week Jeremy started to get little spiky feathers. His eyes were still closed.

When Jeremy was two weeks old he looked more like a bird. His feet were very big and his spiky feathers were getting longer.

Now his eyes were open, and he watched everything around him. He still ate lots of food.

Soon he had lots of real feathers and he was
much heavier.

He loved to be cuddled, and he started to
know his name.

He always told us when it was time for more food by squawking loudly. Boy, did he squawk a lot!

Jeremy grew so fast that he was often tired.
At night he liked to watch television, but
he nearly always fell asleep.

Sometimes he didn't want to go to bed.

Once Jeremy came to school with me
for Show and Tell.

Jeremy was so friendly that everyone wanted to take turns holding him. Jeremy really liked this.

Jeremy's new feathers made him very itchy.

By the time he was four weeks old he looked
just like a grown-up kookaburra – but smaller.

Jeremy loved to watch the fish swimming in our fish tank. I wonder if he was thinking how nice they would be for lunch!

Soon Jeremy wanted to fly. He practised flapping his wings but he could not get off the table.

He would wear himself out and then he would have a sleep.

When Jeremy started to fly properly, he crashed into the walls. It was time for him to be outside.

He loved being in the backyard listening to the other birds. He was now six weeks old.

Over the next few days Jeremy started to fly around a lot. The willy wagtails chased him everywhere.

He always came to the back window when it was
time to be fed.

The day before Christmas, Jeremy came to say goodbye. He landed on my shoulder and gave me a kiss.

Then he flew up to the big gum tree in the backyard to sit with two other small kookaburras.

Perhaps they were his brother and sister.

At sunset the three kookaburras flew away together.

That was the last time we saw Jeremy.

We were so glad that Jeremy had grown
up to be a beautiful healthy kookaburra,
and that he had found his family.